This book belongs to

GIANT STEPS
for little people

KENNETH N. TAYLOR

MARK D. TAYLOR

Illustrated by

Kathryn E. Shoemaker

TYNDALE HOUSE PUBLISHERS, INC.   WHEATON, ILLINOIS

Other Children's Books by Kenneth N. Taylor

Big Thoughts for Little People
Good News for Little People
Wise Words for Little People

My First Bible in Pictures
The Bible in Pictures for Little Eyes
The New Testament in Pictures for Little Eyes

All Scripture verses in this book are from *The Living Bible,* © 1971 by Tyndale House Publishers.

Library of Congress Catalog Card Number 85-51787
ISBN 0-8423-1023-1
Text, copyright © 1985 by Kenneth N. Taylor and Mark D. Taylor
Artwork, copyright © 1985 by Kathryn E. Shoemaker
Printed in the United States of America
95   94

12 11 10 9 8 7

A WORD TO PARENTS (and Grandparents)

Little eyes and ears are powerful. What they see and hear at an early age can deeply affect their entire lives. "Give me a child until he is five years old," it has been said, "and I will have directed his life forever." This statement is true. How important it is, then, to fill little minds with life-changing thoughts.

And what can be more important for a child's life than to know God's laws of right and wrong, and the instructions of Jesus about how to please God as told to us in the Sermon on the Mount?

These great truths are here broken into tasty, bite-sized morsels that a very young child can grasp and grow on. Kathryn Shoemaker's wonderful full-color pictures illustrate and enforce these deep truths.

Each page has a little prayer and a Bible verse. Young children can memorize quite easily, so I encourage you to help your child learn these verses. Picture books are soon outgrown, but Bible verses memorized in childhood last for a lifetime.

Pray with me that God will use this book to help your child, grandchild, or young friend "grow in the grace of our Lord Jesus Christ."

KENNETH N. TAYLOR

P.S. Don't forget to look for the ladybugs in every picture!

Love your father and your mother
And your brother, sister too.
But most of all and best of all,
Love God, for he loves you.

These children love their father and mother. God wants families to love each other. But I will tell you a secret. This family loves God even more than they love each other! And that's exactly what God wants. There are many reasons we should love God and thank him. Most of all, we love him because he loves us. You can thank him for giving you your wonderful parents. You can thank him for giving you enough good food to eat every day, and time to play, and friends. You should thank him for all these good things, and love him all the time.

SOME QUESTIONS TO ANSWER

1. Do these children love their father and mother? How can you tell?
2. Whom should we love more than anyone else?
3. What are some things you can thank God for?

A LITTLE PRAYER

Dear God, help me to love you very much all the time.

A BIBLE VERSE FOR YOU TO LEARN

Love the Lord your God with all your heart, soul, and mind. MATTHEW

Jesus said to love your neighbors.
Help them if you can,
Both now and as you grow to be
A lady or a man.

These people are Christmas caroling. It must be cold, because the children are wearing hats and scarves. Is the weather cold and snowy at Christmas where you live? It looks like the children are singing for their neighbors. This is wonderful, for Jesus said we should love our neighbors as much as we love ourselves. Can you name the people who live near you? They are your neighbors, and you should love them. Jesus wants you to love everyone you know. This is important to remember every day.

SOME QUESTIONS TO ANSWER
1. When we help each other, does this make God glad?
2. Can you name someone who is your neighbor?
3. How can you help him or her?

A LITTLE PRAYER
Dear Lord, help me to love everyone I know.

A BIBLE VERSE FOR YOU TO LEARN
Love your neighbor as much as you love yourself. MATTHEW 22:39

Some kids think they're very smart,
And then start feeling proud.
But all we have has come from God,
So don't be proud and loud.

The girl in the lookout tower thinks she is bigger and better than anyone else. She doesn't know something very important, and I'll tell you what it is. God doesn't like us to be proud and think we are better than other people. He wants us to realize he has made us just the way we are. If you can do something well, thank God for it. Don't act like a big shot. Each of us is better in some things and not as good in others. Each of us should thank God and not be proud.

SOME QUESTIONS TO ANSWER
1. Does God want you to be proud and think you are better than other people?
2. What are you good at doing? (Swimming? Picking up toys?)
3. Who made you better in doing some things and not as good in others?

A LITTLE PRAYER
Dear Father in heaven, thank you for making me good at _____ .

A BIBLE VERSE FOR YOU TO LEARN
Humble men are very fortunate, for the Kingdom of Heaven is given to

…hem. MATTHEW 5:3

Are you sad and lonely?
Do you want a better way?
Ask God to make you happy;
He can do it right away.

I see a little girl who is very sad. She is thinking about something that has happened that makes her sad. I wonder what it is. But she can be happy again. God can make her happy if she asks him to. He can make her realize how many nice things have happened to her. And she can be glad because God loves her. The next time you see someone who is sad, be God's little helper and go and cheer him up. Then three people will be happy —you, the person you have helped, and God will be happy too.

SOME QUESTIONS TO ANSWER
1. What do you think the girl is sad about?
2. Have you been sad today? What happened?
3. Tell about something you can do that helps you feel better when you are sad.

A LITTLE PRAYER
Dear God, thank you that you want to comfort me when I am sad.

A BIBLE VERSE FOR YOU TO LEARN
Those who mourn are fortunate, for they shall be comforted. MATTHEW

15 : 4

Gentleness is always good
Along with your rough play.
So even if you're big and strong
Be thoughtful every day.

Look at all the animals in the pet shop. How many of them can you name? I see rabbits and puppies, fish and chicks. I wonder if the giant birds are real or if they are toys! The children are treating the animals very gently. God wants us to be gentle with people, too. We shouldn't push them around or act like bullies. Instead, we should always try to help one another. Sometimes this is hard to remember, especially if someone pushes you first. But you can ask God to help you respond kindly, even if someone is mean to you.

SOME QUESTIONS TO ANSWER

1. What animals do you see in the picture? Can you see any ladybugs?
2. Are you bigger and stronger than someone else you know? Who is it?
3. Should you get what you want by taking it away from someone who isn't as strong as you are?

A LITTLE PRAYER

Dear God, my Father in heaven, please help me to be kind and gentle to others.

A BIBLE VERSE FOR YOU TO LEARN

The meek and lowly are fortunate, for the whole wide world belongs

to them. MATTHEW 5:5

If you do what's right and just
Because you really care,
Then God will smile,
  because he wants
To see you do what's fair.

Can you find all the children and bears who are hiding? The girl standing behind the tree is counting while the others hide. Is she watching the others while she counts? I hope not. That's not the way to play the game. If she is watching where the others hide, she is cheating. Did you know God can see you all the time—even when you are playing? He is in heaven, but he is also right here in this room. He is happy when you are doing good things, but he is unhappy when you are unfair. I hope you always try to make him happy by doing what is right.

SOME QUESTIONS TO ANSWER
1. Is God here in the room with us?
2. How can you make God happy?
3. What did you do today to make him happy?
   Did you do anything to make him sad?

A LITTLE PRAYER
Dear Father in heaven, please help me always to be fair.

A BIBLE VERSE FOR YOU TO LEARN
Happy are those who long to be just and good, for they shall be com

letely satisfied. MATTHEW 5:6

Acting kind to others
After they've been bad to you
Means you are showing mercy,
And God is happy, too.

Oh my! Look at the huge mess. The girls were having a tea party, but now everything is on the floor. It looks like the boy's truck bumped into the table. I can tell the boy is sorry about the accident, and two of the girls are comforting him. They are saying, "It's all right. It was an accident. We'll help you pick everything up." I'm glad they didn't get angry with him. They are being merciful. You can be merciful by forgiving someone who has hurt you instead of trying to get even. God wants you to be merciful.

SOME QUESTIONS TO ANSWER
1. Point to the girls in the picture who are being kind and merciful.
2. What does it mean to be merciful?
3. Have you ever been merciful? Tell about a time when you helped someone who had been bad to you.

A LITTLE PRAYER
Dear God, help me to be kind to others, even when they have not been kind to me.

A BIBLE VERSE FOR YOU TO LEARN
Happy are the kind and merciful, for they shall be shown mercy.

MATTHEW 5:7

Programs on TV are sometimes good,
But often bad.
Don't watch or read of evil things,
For that will make God sad.

Look at the children watching TV. The little bear is hiding his eyes. He knows it isn't good to watch people who are being bad. If we watch them, we might decide to copy them and be bad too. Sometimes it seems like fun to be naughty, but God doesn't want us to do wrong things. He wants us to do what's right and kind and good. It is easier to do what's right when we think about good things. I'm glad most of the children are playing games or reading good books instead of watching the bad people on TV.

SOME QUESTIONS TO ANSWER

1. Why isn't the bear looking at the television?
2. Do you ever see anyone being bad on TV?
3. What do you think you should do when this happens?

A LITTLE PRAYER

Father in heaven, please help me always to do what's right and kind and good.

A BIBLE VERSE FOR YOU TO LEARN

Happy are those whose hearts are pure, for they shall see God.

MATTHEW 5:8

Don't get into arguments,
Just turn and walk away.
And try to help your friends
 have peace
In both their work and play.

What's going on here? There seems to be a war. The bears have been quarreling with one another, and now they are going to fight. What do you think the boy is telling the bears? I believe he's trying to get them to stop fighting. He wants them to be peaceful. God wants us to be peaceful, too. He doesn't want us to fight with our brothers or sisters or friends. And he wants us to keep others from fighting. He wants us to be peacemakers. He wants all of us to work and play happily together.

SOME QUESTIONS TO ANSWER
1. What are the bears in the picture doing?
2. What is the boy doing?
3. Does God want us to fight or to be peacemakers?

A LITTLE PRAYER
Please, dear God, help me not to quarrel. Help other people not to quarrel either.

A BIBLE VERSE FOR YOU TO LEARN
Happy are those who strive for peace—they shall be called the sons of

God. MATTHEW 5:9

Sometimes you'll be laughed at When you try to do what's right; But God is watching all you do And he approves the sight.

I see someone doing something very naughty. The children are dumping over all the trash cans. Now the garbage is all over the street and the children have made the garbage collector's job very hard. They think it is fun to be bad. They told the girl to help them, but she won't do it. They laughed at her for being good. But the girl and the bears don't care. They want to please God instead of pleasing the other children. God is glad that the girl is obeying him and doing what is good.

SOME QUESTIONS TO ANSWER
1. What are the children doing?
2. Do you think God can see this big mess?
3. Are the girl and the bears going to be naughty too?

A LITTLE PRAYER
Dear God, help me always to do what is right, even if other people laugh at me.

A BIBLE VERSE FOR YOU TO LEARN

Happy are those who are persecuted because they are good, for the

Kingdom of Heaven is theirs.   MATTHEW 5:10

If you say that you love God,
Some kids may laugh and jeer.
But don't let it upset you;
Just remember God is near.

Can you see all the people walking to church? But look! Four of the children are walking in the other direction. They are making fun of the people who are going to church and are telling them not to go. Perhaps they don't know that God would like them to go to church too. I'm glad no one is obeying those children. Sometimes it is very hard to do the right thing if others laugh at us. But we should ask God to help us do what is right. He will help us, even if others are making fun of us.

SOME QUESTIONS TO ANSWER
1. Where are most of the children going?
2. What are the other children doing?
3. Which children are making God glad?

A LITTLE PRAYER
Dear God, help me always to do right, even when others want me to do wrong.

A BIBLE VERSE FOR YOU TO LEARN
When you are laughed at because you are my followers—wonderful!

MATTHEW 5:11

Always try to do what's right,
And never do what's wrong.
Then others who are
watching you
Will sing a happy song.

These children are helping in the garden. They all seem happy, and no one is being naughty or mean. They are doing what is right because they love God and want to please him. The neighbors are watching the children. I believe the neighbors will want to love God when they see how kind the children are to one another. But if children who love God are naughty or mean to one another, others will not want to love God. Often people pay more attention to what we do than what we say.

SOME QUESTIONS TO ANSWER

1. If you are unfriendly or naughty, will your friends want to become God's children?
2. Do you think the neighbors in the picture will want to love God?
3. How can you help other children want to love God?

A LITTLE PRAYER

Dear God, I want to be a good example to others in all I do.

A BIBLE VERSE FOR YOU TO LEARN

Let your good deeds glow for all to see, so that they will praise your

heavenly Father. MATTHEW 5:16

God wants you to share with others
All he's given you.
So give your money cheerfully,
And share your playthings too.

These children are bringing toys and boxes and cans of food to church! Are they going to have a picnic? No, the food is for families who do not have enough money to buy all the food they need. We can show we love God by giving food and toys to people who can't buy their own. We can also give some of our money to God by giving it to our church. Then some of the money will be used to send teachers to tell people about God and his love. Jesus said we should not love our money. We should use some of it to help others.

SOME QUESTIONS TO ANSWER
1. What are the children doing?
2. What will happen to the food?
3. Does God want us to use some of our money to help other people?

A LITTLE PRAYER
Our Father in heaven, thank you that we can help people who don't have enough food.

A BIBLE VERSE FOR YOU TO LEARN
Store treasures in heaven where they will never lose their value, and

are safe from thieves. MATTHEW 6:20

Worry means to think about Bad things that might come true. But God wants you to trust him; He will show you what to do.

It would be nice if no one ever got sick or hurt. But sometimes a child has a temperature or breaks an arm or leg. Does God know about it when you are sick or hurt? Yes! He is always looking down from heaven in love. Sometimes he keeps you from getting hurt, but sometimes he lets you get hurt! Either way he loves you just as much. If he lets you get hurt, does that mean he doesn't love you? Of course not! He loves you all the time, and he will be with you and help you all the time, even when you are sick or hurt.

SOME QUESTIONS TO ANSWER
1. What is happening in the picture?
2. Does God love you even when he lets you get sick or hurt?
3. Should you thank him for loving you all the time? Let's do it now.

A LITTLE PRAYER
Dear God, thank you for loving me and being with me all the time, even when I am sick or hurt.

A BIBLE VERSE FOR YOU TO LEARN
Don't be anxious about tomorrow.   God will take care of your tomo

ow too. Live one day at a time. MATTHEW 6:34

God can hear you praying,
Whether morning, noon, or night.
He answers, "Yes,"
or answers, "No."
He knows what's best and right.

What is this family doing? That's right, they are praying. Perhaps the children are thanking God for their mother and father, and for their friends, and for a fun day. They may be thanking God, or they may be asking him for something they want. Sometimes God gives us exactly what we ask for, but sometimes he says, "It wouldn't be good for you to have what you are asking for!" Then God will say, "No" or "Not yet." We can trust God to give us what is good and not give us what is bad for us, even if we want it and ask him for it.

SOME QUESTIONS TO ANSWER

1. What do you think the children are talking to God about?
2. Does God always give us what we ask him for? What if we ask for something that is not good for us?
3. What are you thankful for?

A LITTLE PRAYER

Father in heaven, thank you that you always know what is best for me.

A BIBLE VERSE FOR YOU TO LEARN

Ask and it will be given to you. MATTHEW 7:7

How should you treat others?
I will tell you what to do.
Be kind and also helpful,
Just as you want done to you.

These children are having a happy time on the merry-go-round. But I see something I don't like. A big boy is grabbing a balloon away from a little boy. Is that a good way for him to act? Of course not! How do you think the big boy would like it if somebody did that to him? He wouldn't like it at all. God tells us not to do anything to others we wouldn't want them to do to us. We should be as kind to others as we want them to be to us. That's the way God wants us to act.

SOME QUESTIONS TO ANSWER

1. Look at the picture and point to some children who are being kind. What are they doing?
2. Which boy is doing something naughty? What is he doing?
3. Do you want people to be nice to you? How should you treat them?

A LITTLE PRAYER

Dear Lord, help me to treat others just as I want them to treat me.

A BIBLE VERSE FOR YOU TO LEARN

Do for others what you want them to do for you. MATTHEW 7:12

Once I built a castle;
I was pleased as I could be.
But then the waves got bigger,
And they washed it out to sea.

Have you ever been to the beach and played in the sand? Maybe
you built a castle with wet sand, and then a big wave came
and knocked it down! That's what is happening in the picture.
The children have spent a long time building their castle,
but now it is all going to fall down. Too bad! But look at the
children who are building a castle on the rocks. The water
will not knock it down. Those children are wise. Jesus says you
are wise, too, if you do whatever God tells you to do. You
are like the wise children who are building their castle on the
rocks.

SOME QUESTIONS TO ANSWER
1. What happens when waves hit a sand castle?
2. Are the children wise to build a castle on the rocks? Why?
3. Are you wise when you do whatever God wants you to do?

A LITTLE PRAYER
Dear God in heaven, I want to be wise and do what you want
me to do.

A BIBLE VERSE FOR YOU TO LEARN
All who listen to my instructions and follow them are wise, like a man

who builds his house on solid rock. MATTHEW 7:24

The Bible is the Word of God,
Its stories all are true.
If you can't read,
   I'm sure your mom
Or dad will read to you.

Can you see what is happening in the picture? The children's father is reading a book to them. It's a very special book filled with stories from the Bible. The Bible has many wonderful true stories about people who lived many years ago. It tells us about God and about God's love for us. And the Bible tells us how God wants us to live. The Bible is the most important book ever written. Someday you will be able to read the Bible for yourself. God likes it when we read the Bible.

SOME QUESTIONS TO ANSWER
1. What is the name of God's very special book?
2. What does the Bible tell us about?
3. Can you think of any stories from the Bible?

A LITTLE PRAYER
Dear God, thank you for the Bible. Please help me do what it tells me to do.

A BIBLE VERSE FOR YOU TO LEARN
The whole Bible was given to us by inspiration from God. 2 TIMOTHY

3:16

Once I knew a little girl
Who liked to storm and pout.
If she's not careful, other kids
Will want to leave her out.

Do you see the little girl who is lying on the ground crying? I'm afraid she's making a big fuss about nothing. Do you ever do that? I hope not! God wants you to be happy. Here is what the little girl should do. She should stop crying and she should think about something nice. She could think about the nice friends God has given her, or she could think about her wonderful family. God has given her so much to be happy about. You talk to her now and tell her to be happy instead of mad. Say to her, "Little girl, please be happy because God loves you."

SOME QUESTIONS TO ANSWER

1. What are the children on the stage doing?
2. Why is the girl on the ground unhappy?
3. How can she be happy?

A LITTLE PRAYER

Dear Lord, help me to be happy all the time.

A BIBLE VERSE FOR YOU TO LEARN

Whatever happens, dear friends, be glad in the Lord. PHILIPPIANS 3:1

God made all the grass and birds,
The stars and moon and sun.
We worship him because he's God,
The great and mighty one.

At night when you look up into the sky, you can see the moon and stars. In the day you can see the sun. God made all these things, and he made the flowers and grass and you and me. But some children don't know about God. They don't know he made all these things, and they don't know God loves them. Some children in other countries think there are many gods, but there is really only one God. He made everything. Missionaries go to tell people about God. Maybe someday you can go and tell them too.

SOME QUESTIONS TO ANSWER
1. What do you see when you look into the sky at night?
2. Who made the moon and stars?
3. Is there more than one God?

A LITTLE PRAYER
Dear God, I know you are the only God there is. Thank you that you love me.

A BIBLE VERSE FOR YOU TO LEARN
You may worship no other god than me. EXODUS 20:3

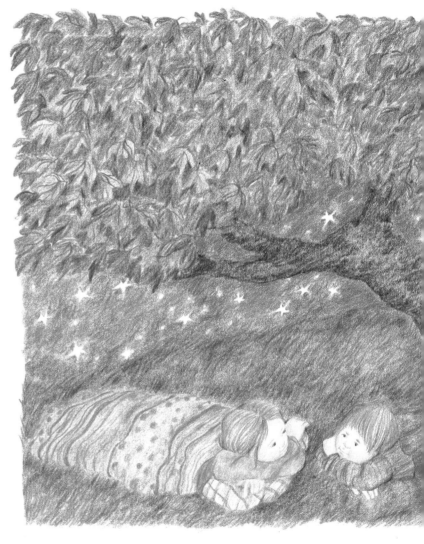

Idols made of wood or stone
Can't walk or talk or call.
We should not make or worship them,
For they're not God at all.

Do you know what an idol is? It is a piece of wood or stone carved to look like a bird or animal, or like a man or woman. You can see a picture of an idol in the book the mother is holding. The sad thing about idols is that some people in other countries think idols are alive! They bring gifts to the idols and pray to them! But God doesn't like this at all, because idols are not God and no one should ever pray to them. We must only worship the true God and never worship anything else. We need to go and tell the people who worship idols about the one true God.

SOME QUESTIONS TO ANSWER

1. Where is the idol in the picture?
2. Should people worship idols?
3. Whom should we worship?

A LITTLE PRAYER

Dear Father in heaven, help me always to worship only you.

A BIBLE VERSE FOR YOU TO LEARN

You shall not make any idols. EXODUS 20:4

God's name is very holy;
Do not use it as a curse.
Though dirty words should not be used,
To swear is even worse.

One of the boys in the picture is saying something very naughty, and the girl and the bears are holding their ears so they won't hear it. The boy is mad at his blocks and he said, "Oh, God!" but he wasn't thinking about God at all. That is wrong, and God says never to do it. His name is holy. It must be respected and honored, and not used carelessly. You can use God's name when you pray and when you are telling others about him, but not when you are just playing. Please remember this because it is so important to God.

SOME QUESTIONS TO ANSWER
1. What is happening in the picture?
2. Why are the bears holding their ears?
3. Should you say God's name or use naughty words when you are angry?

A LITTLE PRAYER
Dear Father in heaven, help me always to honor your holy name.

A BIBLE VERSE FOR YOU TO LEARN
You shall not use the name of Jehovah your God irreverently.   EXODUS

20:7

Seven days are in each week,
But one's a special day.
And on that day we go to church
To worship and to pray.

The children's choir is singing songs of thanks and praise to God. When God created the world he gave us a special day of rest every week. He wants his people to stop their work and take time to think about him. He tells us to meet together with others of his people, and pray together and sing his praises and learn from the Bible and talk about God's love. Some people forget to do this, or else they don't care about what God wants. I hope you make God happy by going to church every week.

SOME QUESTIONS TO ANSWER
1. What are the children in the picture doing?
2. Can you name the seven days of the week?
3. Which one is a special day to rest and go to church?

A LITTLE PRAYER
Dear God, thank you that we can go to church to worship you.

A BIBLE VERSE FOR YOU TO LEARN
Remember to observe the Sabbath as a holy day. EXODUS 20:8

God says to obey your parents;
Do it with a smile.
So don't be grouchy, mad, or sad—
Try smiling for a while.

Look what a nice thing these children are doing! They have
made breakfast for their father and mother and are serving it to
them while they are still in bed. The children are honoring
their parents. They are showing their love and respect. In the
Bible God tells children to obey their fathers and mothers.
That means doing what they tell you to do without getting
grouchy or talking back. Your parents know what is best for you
and what is dangerous or wrong. So you must obey and
honor them. That makes God very happy.

SOME QUESTIONS TO ANSWER
1. What are the children doing?
2. Why are they doing it?
3. Should you talk back to your parents?

A LITTLE PRAYER
Dear God, help me to honor and obey my mother and father
even when I don't feel like it.

A BIBLE VERSE FOR YOU TO LEARN
Honor your father and mother. EXODUS 20:12

Anger can be dangerous,
For it can make you bad.
So turn it off and then forgive,
And that will make God glad.

The children in the picture are throwing rocks and trying to hurt each other. The bears are hiding behind the trees. They know it is wrong for the children to do this. I'm sorry the children don't know this too. If you see someone in a movie or on TV hurting and killing people, say to yourself, "No, that is very wrong." God says we should not kill people. It is wrong to hate people too, even if they have hurt you or done something wrong to you. God says you should forgive them and love them.

SOME QUESTIONS TO ANSWER
1. Why are the bears hiding?
2. Does God want people to kill each other?
3. Is it OK to hate other people?

A LITTLE PRAYER
Dear Father in heaven, please help me not to hate other people, even if they're mean to me.

A BIBLE VERSE FOR YOU TO LEARN
You must not murder. EXODUS 20:13

A boy grows up, becomes a man, And then he gets a wife. The Bible says that they should stay Together all their life.

Oh, look! It's a wedding! Everyone is happy and excited. Do you see the children's parents standing there watching? God gives mothers and fathers to one another to take care of each other and to take care of their children. God knows it is best for children to have both a mother and a father, so he tells parents always to keep on loving each other. Sometimes fathers or mothers don't obey God and don't love each other anymore, but that makes God unhappy. So if you get married, always love your husband or wife and not someone else instead.

SOME QUESTIONS TO ANSWER

1. Does God want mothers and fathers always to love each other?
2. How can you tell that the parents in the picture love each other?
3. If you get married when you grow up, will you always love your husband or wife?

A LITTLE PRAYER

Dear God, please help mothers and fathers everywhere to keep on loving each other.

A BIBLE VERSE FOR YOU TO LEARN

You must not commit adultery. EXODUS 20:14

When you're older you will find
That some kids like to steal.
They hide the gum and slip away—
How sad that makes God feel.

Oh, no! I see a girl stealing some candy. She is putting it in her purse instead of paying for it. The lady at the candy counter isn't looking. But someone is watching. God sees the girl doing this, and he is very sad. Did you ever take something that wasn't yours, and hide it? I hope not, for that is stealing. If you have stolen something, please give it back and tell the person you are sorry. Then tell God you are sorry. He will forgive you. God is glad when we obey him by not stealing.

SOME QUESTIONS TO ANSWER
1. What kind of store is in the picture?
2. What does stealing mean? Who in the picture is stealing?
3. Is it OK to steal things from a store?

A LITTLE PRAYER
Dear God, help me never to take things that don't belong to me.

A BIBLE VERSE FOR YOU TO LEARN
You must not steal. EXODUS 20:15

Tell the truth no matter what;
It's best at any time.
For telling lies just makes things
  worse;
It really is a crime.

Can you see that a cookie is missing from the cookie pan? I wonder where it is? Oh, now I see it! Look what the boy is holding behind his back! His big sister is asking him if he took it, and I'm sorry to say he's telling a lie. He is saying he did not take it. God is very unhappy when his children don't tell the truth. Why is the boy afraid to tell the truth? I think it's because he knows he will be scolded or punished. But he should be brave and do what is right and say, "Yes, I took it." I hope he doesn't lie again.

SOME QUESTIONS TO ANSWER
1. Where is the cookie?
2. What is a lie?
3. Does God want us to tell lies?

A LITTLE PRAYER
Dear Father in heaven, help me to remember always to tell the truth.

A BIBLE VERSE FOR YOU TO LEARN
You must not lie. EXODUS 20:16

Thank the Lord for all you have;
Then if the neighbor boys
Get newer trucks or bigger trikes,
You'll still like your own toys.

Have you ever wished you had a toy that belongs to your friend? The Bible says it isn't good to want other people's things. God wants you to be happy with what you have, instead of being sad about things you don't have. In the picture you can see a little girl with a wagon who wants a Bigwheel instead. She is angry because her friend has a Bigwheel and she doesn't. But God doesn't always let you have everything you want. You should thank him for everything you have instead of being sorry you don't have more.

SOME QUESTIONS TO ANSWER
1. What does the girl in the picture wish she had?
2. Should you be sorry and mad if someone has a nicer toy than you have?
3. Are you thankful for all the nice things you have? What are some of them?

A LITTLE PRAYER
Dear God, thank you for giving me so many nice things.

A BIBLE VERSE FOR YOU TO LEARN

You must not be envious of your neighbor's house ... or anything else

he has. EXODUS 20:17

ABOUT THE AUTHORS

Kenneth N. Taylor is best known as the translator of *The Living Bible*, but his first renown was as a writer of children's books. Ken and his wife, Margaret, have ten children, and his early books were written for use in the family's daily devotions. The manuscripts were ready for publication only when they passed the scrutiny of those ten young critics! Those books, which have now been read to two generations of children around the world, include *The Bible in Pictures for Little Eyes* (Moody Press), *Stories for the Children's Hour* (Moody Press), and *Taylor's Bible Story Book* (Tyndale House). Now the Taylor children are all grown, so *Giant Steps for Little People* and *Big Thoughts for Little People* were written with the numerous grandchildren in mind.

Ken Taylor is a graduate of Wheaton College and Northern Baptist Seminary. He is the founder and chairman of Tyndale House Publishers, Inc. He and Margaret live in Wheaton, Illinois.

Mark D. Taylor is one of the ten children for whom Ken's earlier books were written. Mark is the president of Tyndale House Publishers, and he and his wife, Carol, have five rambunctious children of their own.

ABOUT THE ILLUSTRATOR

Kathryn E. Shoemaker has had broad experience as an art teacher, curriculum specialist, filmmaker, and illustrator. Her published works include fourteen books, eight filmstrips, illustrations for many magazine articles, and numerous educational in-service materials. She is a strong advocate of the involvement of parents in the local schools, and spends a great deal of time as a volunteer in her children's school. She is also a volunteer with the Canadian Mental Health Association and the Red Cross.

Kathryn is a graduate of Immaculate Heart College in Los Angeles. She also studied at Chouinards Art Institute, Otis Art Institute, and Occidental College, and is a member of the Society of Illustrators. She and her two children, Kristen and Andrew, who helped critique the illustrations for *Giant Steps for Little People*, live in Vancouver, British Columbia.